# This Is My

### Betty Kwong Lee

### Illustrated by Chi Chung

## Rigby®

A Harcourt Achieve Imprint

www.Rigby.com
1-800-531-5015

My name is Jen Moy.

This is my family.

This is my father.
This is my mother.

5

This is my grandfather.
He likes to help me
with my bicycle.

This is my grandmother.
She likes to cook.

This is my sister Yun.
She likes to read.

11

"Big Sister, can I have this paper?" I say.

"Yes, you can," says Yun.

13

"Big Sister, can I have the markers?" I say.

"Yes, you can," Yun says.

14

This is my family!